Sugar Lump's
Night Before Christmas

Sugar Lump's
Night Before Christmas

by Lynn Sheffield Simmons

illustrated by
Sue Marshall Ward

Pelican Publishing Company
GRETNA 2007

*The word "Pelican" and the depiction of a pelican
are trademarks of Pelican Publishing Company, Inc.,
and are registered in the U.S. Patent and Trademark Office.*

Library of Congress Cataloging-in-Publication Data

Simmons, Lynn Sheffield.
  Sugar Lump's night before Christmas / Lynn Sheffield
Simmons ; illustrated by Sue Marshall Ward.
     p. cm.
  Based on Clement Moore's Night before Christmas.
  ISBN 978-1-58980-439-5 (alk. paper)
  1. Calves—Juvenile poetry. 2. Santa Claus—Juvenile poet-
ry. 3. Christmas stories. 4. Children's poetry, American. I.
Ward, Sue Marshall, 1941- ill. II. Moore, Clement Clarke,
1779-1863. Night before Christmas. III. Title.
  PS3569.I4737S84 2007
  811'.6—dc22

                                        2007011787

Printed in Singapore
Published by Pelican Publishing Company, Inc.
1000 Burmaster Street, Gretna, Louisiana 70053

To Larry

'Twas the night before Christmas
on the Simmonses' farm.
The cows huddled together,
trying to stay warm.

A small calf shivered
alone on the path.
He was known as Sugar Lump,
the orphan calf.

His snowy white face
with black circling one eye
Shined in the night
as he looked at the sky.

The cows watched and wondered
who Santa would pick
to pull his big sled,
for his reindeer were sick.

"He'll pick us,"
the brown cows bawled.
"It'll be us,"
the longhorns drawled.

"It'll be me!" said Sugar Lump
in a loud bellow.
"I can help Santa!"
yelled the spunky little fellow.

"Soon Santa will come
with a lot of toys
for the cows to deliver
to good girls and boys."

Suddenly, eight sneezing reindeer
came pulling a sled,
wanting to hurry home
and get into bed.

"Let's hurry," wheezed the driver
all dressed in red.
His voice was a whisper:
"It's a head cold," he said.

He unhitched the reindeer,
this short, chubby man.
Pointing out cows,
he then began.

He chose four longhorns
all huddled together,
then four other cows
in the cold Texas weather.

"Pick me! Please pick me!"
Sugar Lump begged,
unhappy that Santa
took the others instead.

"You're too young,"
said Santa in a hoarse voice,
feeling sad that he had
no other choice.

"You have to be strong
to pull that big sled.
It's very hard work,"
all the cows said.

"I can do it!" Sugar Lump wailed,
trying not to show tears.
He yelled so loud
the cows covered their ears.

Santa hitched up the cows
and sat down for the flight
to deliver his toys
on this Christmas Eve night.

Then looking at Sugar Lump,
Santa stroked his chin.
"Do you know these cows' names?"
he asked with a grin.

"Yes, sir, I do,"
he said, feeling neglected,
then shouted the names
that Santa selected:

"Molly, Suzy,
Joseph, and Ed,
Bully, Winston,
Clarence, and Ned!"

As Sugar Lump shouted,
calling out all their names,
the cows lunged forward
and pulled at the reins.

"Hop in," said Santa,
pushing presents aside.
Sugar Lump was excited.
"I can go!" he cried.

"You'll be my voice," whispered Santa
on this cold Christmas Eve,
as Sugar Lump stood by him
all ready to leave.

Santa loosened the reins
as Sugar Lump called,
"Get going, cows—
let's get this sled hauled!"

They ran over the prairie
as fast as could be,
taking off in the air,
sailing over a tree.

Sugar Lump shouted
as they started their flight,
"Merry Christmas to all
and to all a good night!"